BOA

Clara Brennan

BOA

OBERON BOOKS
LONDON

WWW.OBERONBOOKS.COM

First published in 2015 by Oberon Books Ltd
521 Caledonian Road, London N7 9RH
Tel: +44 (0.) 20 7607 3637 / Fax: +44 (0.) 20 7607 3629
e-mail: info@oberonbooks.com
www.oberonbooks.com

A catalogue record for this book is available from the British
Library.

PB ISBN: 978-1-78319-211-3
E ISBN: 978-1-78319-710-1

Cover photography by Helen Murray
Artwork and design by Tim Jarmain-Groves for Graphic Design
London

Printed and bound by Marston Book Services, Didcot.

Visit www.oberonbooks.com to read more about all our books
and to buy them. You will also find features, author interviews and
news of any author events, and you can sign up for e-newsletters
so that you're always first to hear about our new releases.

For Mum and Dad.

Thank you to Hannah, Harriet and Guy for making the play, to Caitlin Albery Beavan, Aron Rollin, Jessica Cooper, Kat Buckle, Camilla Young, Marianne Buckland, Pauline Lord, Anna Starkey, Katy Wix, Clare Suart, Bob Capers, Bradford Bailey, Nina Steiger, George Spender and all at Oberon, Steven Atkinson, Francesca Clark, Holly Kendrick and all at HighTide Festival, Annie & Richie Price, Anne & Urquhart Neilson, Craig Neilson, Sean Durkin and my family.

Boa was first performed as a reading at Hightide Festival on 13 April 2014.

It premiered at Trafalgar Studios 2 on 5 February 2015, with the following cast:

BOA   Harriet Walter

LOUIS   Guy Paul

Written by Clara Brennan

Directed by Hannah Price

Set Designer Anthony Lamble

Costume Designer Jenny Beavan

Lighting Designer Malcolm Rippeth

Music & Sound Designer Dave Price

Movement Director Ann Yee

Choreographer Michela Meazza

Wardrobe Supervisor Kat Smith

General Manager Tom Miller

Production Assistant Ingrid Hinojosa

Stage Manager Marie Costa

Company Stage Manager Sunita Hinduja

Assistant Stage Manager Katrina Mansfield

Produced by Caitlin Albery Beavan and Aron Rollin for Moya Productions.

Characters

BOA

LOUIS

Settings include:

A Bowery kitchen, New York City, 1980s

A house in Belmont, New Hampshire, 1980s

Backstage at a New York City dance performance, tonight

A flat in Little Venice, London, 1990s

A house in Maida Vale, London 1990s

A hotel room in Phnom Penh, 2000s

Whitechapel Hospital, London 2000s

Another category

1.

LOUIS:	How you doin', Belinda?
BOA:	What are you doing back here?
LOUIS:	I'm checking up on you.
BOA:	You never called me that.
LOUIS:	I did. Whenever you called me a Smug/
LOUIS AND BOA:	Yankee Bastard.
BOA:	Why now? Louis?
	LOUIS shrugs.
LOUIS:	You know, once, at a work party someone asked me about your nickname. I said: 'I know! God knows how they got from Belinda to that diminutive!'
BOA:	You know my brother couldn't say it/
LOUIS:	I told the guy sometimes your arm around my neck felt like…a feather boa…and sometimes it felt like a big ol' snake. Squeezing the life outta me. God, you look good.
BOA:	As do you.
LOUIS:	I've loved you since the moment I saw you.
BOA:	So you always said.
LOUIS:	Drinking alone?
BOA:	No: special occasion. Join me!
LOUIS:	I'm teetotal these days.
BOA:	Bully for you.

1

LOUIS:	Boa.
BOA:	No.
LOUIS:	I hear you gotta show out there?
BOA:	You'll hate it.
LOUIS:	Try me.
BOA:	It's inspired by the traditional *cueca* duet that the wives of the disappeared in Chile have danced solo, as a form of protest and lamentation.
LOUIS:	It sounds beautiful, I can't wait to see it!
BOA:	Bastard.
LOUIS:	No, I love that *political dance* is still a *thing!*
BOA:	As ever Louis, you are unable to comprehend the deep, internal wisdom that bodies contain.
LOUIS:	Well quick let's go out there and watch them leaping about! In a show inspired by a totalitarian regime, or genocide! And then we'll go home and forget all about it!
BOA:	I know I'm privileged to be talking about human rights in the abstract! Lucky me! Spending my days pondering distant wars, pondering *those* children dying eleven hours from me, and then…oh! Then I cut into an avocado and the avocado is bad it's rotten inside and I think…'oh my god there is nothing worse in this whole world than waiting for an avocado to ripen and then cutting into it and finding it's bad!'
LOUIS:	Boa. I've got something to tell you.

BOA: I can't stand it

LOUIS: Your own privilege?

BOA: Oh fuck off. No your – piss-taking.

He's sorry.

BOA: Have I got red wine lips?

LOUIS: Little bit.

BOA: You think when you were a reporter you didn't write fiction?

LOUIS: Ahh – yep – here we go!

BOA: They call articles stories for a reason – you have to add human details, description.

LOUIS: The detail is all too human.

BOA: But non-fiction still has a narrative. If it didn't, the history books would just be a numerical timeline with no story at all!

LOUIS: Ooh, very good, thought that one through!

BOA: I have missed wanting to kill you!

LOUIS: Boa, journalists chase the present for the truth: I never said they find it! It's historians who add the flab/

BOA: Aghhh! All these years Louis, and you still think the mind is in the brain!

LOUIS: Where else would it be?

BOA: In the heart, in the toes! Fingertips/

LOUIS: Inner thighs?

BOA:	Oh well I forget…yours is definitely in your pants!
LOUIS:	My brain is in my pants?
BOA:	Well, in your knickers.
LOUIS:	I don't wear knickers: I'm an American.
BOA:	Oh fuck off!
LOUIS:	And a man/
BOA:	Oh do have a drink, Louis!

LOUIS waves his hands to decline.

LOUIS:	You can drink for two.
BOA:	What did you want to tell me? I need you to be gone when the show comes down.

2.

LOUIS:	You saved my life.
BOA:	Rubbish! When did I?!
LOUIS:	1981. Right here in Manhattan.
BOA:	I never saved anyone's life.
LOUIS:	When I first met you I thought you were a stuck up, prissy English schoolgirl with a rod up your ass.
BOA:	I can take that.
LOUIS:	I was having a *liaison* with your roommate.

BOA: I know! I heard you shagging her before I met you!

LOUIS: You did not!

BOA: I did! I lay there with my Walkman on full blast! I was expecting a Quarterback to emerge from her room!

LOUIS: Well, we had nothing to talk about since your roommate marveled constantly /

BOA: Emily/

LOUIS: at how many books I had read! And then, one day, she told me that she didn't like history/

BOA: You're such a snob!

LOUIS: So I said to her: 'What, not even yesterday?'

BOA: Very droll.

LOUIS: And then I was heading for the exit/

BOA: Ever the young cad/

LOUIS: Except at that moment – you walked into that disgusting kitchen. Swamped, in a tatty old man's bathrobe, with hair dye spattering the collar, a cigarette dangling between your lips, and I'll never forget, you did an impersonation of an old-school film star, and you said:

BOA: 'Good morning Henry! Or Alec! Or Richard or Paul or Max – or Lionel – or *who*ever *the hell* you are.'

LOUIS: And that – was it.

BOA: For you, maybe. I still wished I'd gone to the Netherlands! There, the ballet didn't

	bat an eyelid at you being more than five foot nothing, with all those great big milk-fed Dutch boys to partner! Mm!
LOUIS:	Yes, well. You'd just joined a 'modern' ensemble on the side, and in that first week alone, you subjected me to three evenings and a matinee of the off-off-off-off-practically-in-the-river Broadway experimental dance piece called…'Blood and Honey', or something equally dire! Now what was it about?
BOA:	Migrant workers.
LOUIS:	Migrant workers! Your ballet friends were all wildly hip, and looked on me with mild disdain – tolerated me because I was on the arm of Boa – their British queen. God, the eighties in New York!
BOA:	All my beautiful boys are dead.
LOUIS:	*(A toast.)* To the boys.
	But I tell you, every time I left you back then I was just walking on air. I think now – I've come to believe – that how a person makes you feel when you *leave* them, is a pretty good indication of whether they're good for you. And with you, Boa, I just felt whenever I left you that I could take on the world. You were fearless. And I used to walk away like this. *(He stands tall and broadens.)*
BOA:	I remember that first week – we didn't have sex.
LOUIS:	That's not possible!

BOA:	Yes, because you always went home early! Had to get up to do five hundred laps around Central Park before work?
LOUIS:	I was playing hard to get!
BOA:	I was dying for a shag! But then –
LOUIS:	Dad died.
BOA:	I still wish I'd met him.
LOUIS:	You said I revered him with a kind of blanket romanticism, he wasn't all good, he had his faults, but –
BOA:	You disappeared. Wouldn't let me go to the funeral. So I got on the train to the middle of bloody nowhere.
LOUIS:	Belmont, New Hampshire.

3.

BOA:	I stand in the living room of your father's house in New England. America. And suddenly I think oh you dear, stupid girl, turning up uninvited.
	The place is being redecorated: there's just one armchair and then nailed onto hooks on the wall is a fucking massive yellow/
LOUIS:	Kayak.
BOA:	You kayak down rivers. Rather than drive?
LOUIS:	*(Shrugs.)* Easiest way to get from A to B.

BOA: I mean who does that? *American* boys do that!

LOUIS: Yeah Dad was a backwoodsman. I was the first person in my family to go to college and after Mum died – lymphoma when I was four – he raised me…well, look around you… I guess I grew up pretty much…dirt poor! So did our neighbours… Dad wouldn't buy a belt when I was a boy, I recall… He spent every cent he had getting me through school – so he held his trousers up with twine, with string – I –

BOA: You're in a plaid shirt and jeans, the all American boy with sawdust in your wild pale hair. You have a beard – since back then you couldn't get you near a razor – and those beautiful hands with bitten fingernails, and you've lost weight, and I see the sinews working in your forearms as you nervously roll up your shirt sleeves and roll them down again… I now feel wildly inappropriate because in your grief you look more beautiful than ever! And frankly, all I can think about is shagging your brains out.

LOUIS: I'm renovating the house. I oughta sell it. I'm never here, so.

BOA: A lone wolf. Agghhhh it was awkward! Was it awkward?

LOUIS: It was awkward.

BOA: I'm sort of ready to pounce, but I could feel you getting further and further away from me!

LOUIS:	The goodness of that man, his heart. I think it made me who I am… It sent me looking for… I don't know Boa. Truth? I don't know anything. My head, it's empty.
BOA:	Give me a beer. Just tell me the first thing that comes into your head. The first thing.
LOUIS:	Uhhh. Your nickname…means 'good' in Portuguese.
BOA:	Ha, yes.
LOUIS:	Boa tarde is it? Boa noite – that's Portuguese?
BOA:	But I'm not in the least bit good. I'm the least good person I've ever met.
LOUIS:	That's not true.
BOA:	I know a phrase: voce tem uma boa estrura ossea.
LOUIS:	Which means?
BOA:	You have a really good bone structure.
	A long, awkward pause.
LOUIS:	I'm sorry, I can't think of anything except my Dad and the word orphan – orphan, orphan –
BOA:	He was your home.
LOUIS:	Tell me a story, or something, Boa!
BOA:	I can't…/
LOUIS:	He fell on the stones out there, some kids found him!

He gets up, shakes his hands out, and moves away.

BOA: On the way here/

LOUIS: What?

BOA: As I crossed Washington Square to get the train, I'm hurrying across the square, sweating like mad, and this guy runs up to me and goes: 'This heat dried up my dick, girl! This heat dried up my balls! Now I only got pussy left!' *(They giggle.)* And off he goes on his way! And then – see I attract them, I'm like a magnet for beautiful freaks! On the train – there's this purple-haired lady from Cape Town and she grilled me the whole way. And she said, 'Coming all this way to see him? You must love him.' *(Awkward – she covers.)* and I laughed – and she said 'Well never mind, dear. I'm marrying a lover half my age!' And she said she believed in packing it all in, in Life in Big Bags. And she had such a sense of the things, and oh! I had to promise to tell you 'A purple-haired lady from Cape Town told me to tell you that a purple-haired lady from Cape Town said she believed in Life in Big Bags.'

LOUIS: Big Bags. I like that.

BOA: Me too.

LOUIS: I wanted you…oh Christ of course! I mean this English goddess is sitting on an upturned crate swigging a bottle of beer and you manage to be glamorous in men's jeans and a turtleneck, I mean, you could wear a sack. You're sitting there in

the wreckage of my dead father's house
with this unlit cigarette dangling between
your lips, gesturing with these great long-
fingered dancing Sicilian hands, *(Like
this.),* like some…big…lithe…scary…
cat, and I'm thinking 'I'm going to cry!
I'm going to break down in front of this
incredible woman and she's *not* going to
want to handle it!' I mean I've seen…you
know, even at twenty-seven, in my job,
I've seen some pretty heavy shit, so I'm…
I'm not a crier. But I was going to go any
minute; it was all I could do to not weep
with gratitude that you had found me.

See the rafters? I ripped the cabinets
off the wall and they've built the entire
kitchen around the frame of an old
caboose! The entire room!

BOA: It's… Impressive!

LOUIS: They call that 'Yankee Ingenuity!'

BOA: What's a caboose?

LOUIS: Last car in an old-fashioned steam train?
Has a cupola on the roof so you can see
ahead over the tracks.

BOA: Ahhh, I see!

LOUIS: Native word. And it's slang for 'your ass',
Dad used to say it.

BOA: 'My! What a hot little caboose you have!'

LOUIS: See how they just hauled it in here,
bricked up the windows and then
plastered over it? It must've been my
grandfather! Now what a genius that man
was! He didn't care a damn for aesthetics

– just pull that old caboose in there and you've got an instant extra room! Makes me want to take the rest of the house apart to see how he made it!

BOA: How do you cook if you don't have a kitchen?

LOUIS: You're hungry!

BOA: Oh I didn't mean/

LOUIS: I've got a ham outside, I can roast it? I've made a fire pit.

BOA: I'm a vegetarian.

LOUIS: Aghh, I forgot!

BOA: Sorry.

LOUIS: Damn hippies!

BOA: I've probably got one apple, in my bag –

LOUIS: No, no, I'm joking. I'll make you pancakes!

BOA: You cooked a stack over a fire outside. Wrapped me in a blanket covered in dog hair. Was there a dog?

LOUIS: Jesus, Boa. Hunter: he adored you.

BOA: Hunter. Of course.

LOUIS: Just keep killing those brain cells!

BOA: I'm sorry! I remember him.

LOUIS: Just keep on drowning them!

BOA: All right! I know, you left him with the neighbours and I still regret letting you.

LOUIS: New York is no place for a dog.

BOA:	*(She briskly claps her hands.)* No melancholy!
LOUIS:	So, at some point I slip out for more beers. I run, grinning, down to the car.
BOA:	You go. I look around, and then I go indoors and straight upstairs and there are two bedrooms – and one is your old boyhood bedroom! I know what I'm looking for! You've already won a Pulitzer at twenty-six.
LOUIS:	It's just a fucking Tiffany paperweight.
BOA:	I mean can you imagine anything sexier than a Pulitzer prize-winner with a kayak on his wall? So I'm looking for the fucking Pulitzer, rummaging around your room and I find it under shoeboxes in the bottom of your closet/
LOUIS:	I catch you snooping.
BOA:	Which confirms I'm nuts.
LOUIS:	Hi!
BOA:	Oh, fffffuck.
LOUIS:	You get lost?
BOA:	Yes actually.
LOUIS:	What you got there?
BOA:	Nothin'.
LOUIS:	Nothin'?
BOA:	I was looking for the –
LOUIS:	Bathroom?

BOA:	No I just wanted to see your old – oh bollocks to it, I'm a nosey cow, OK! I knew it'd be here somewhere, I've just never seen one!
LOUIS:	Well I don't keep it on display!
BOA:	Why not?
LOUIS:	I never took it out the box.
BOA:	You silly boy!
LOUIS:	I'm a 'silly boy'?!
BOA:	You should be proud of it!
LOUIS:	I couldn't be less proud.
BOA:	Rubbish!
LOUIS:	Rubbish – there you go! You say rubbish all the time. I wondered then if the English really say rubbish as much as you say rubbish. Now *I* call it rubbish.
BOA:	You won a Pulitzer at the age of twenty-six for East Asia coverage/
LOUIS:	For picking up a pen!
BOA:	And you leave it in a box?
LOUIS:	*(Shrugs.)*
BOA:	It's very pretty. Very heavy. Oop – oo-up – what if I drop it, what if I? *(She pretends to nearly drop it, then to throw it – of course she doesn't.)*
LOUIS:	Hey, hey hey – Here –
BOA:	Ooh up, butterfingers, nearly dropped it, here, catch!
LOUIS:	No –

BOA:	Care about it now, don't you!
LOUIS:	Give it!
BOA:	Very shiny Louis! Are you sure you don't nip up here to polish it?
LOUIS:	Hand it to me/
BOA:	Is it glass or crystal?
LOUIS:	I don't care/
BOA:	It's like a big icicle! Oops nearly went then/
LOUIS:	I'm told they come in all different shapes/
BOA:	I like this one!
LOUIS:	Give it here.
BOA:	No.
LOUIS:	Hand it to me.
BOA:	Take your clothes off.
LOUIS:	What?
BOA:	I'll hold it while you take your clothes off.
LOUIS:	Fine.
BOA:	You fucked me with it.
LOUIS:	Well. It was in the bed.
	They laugh.
BOA:	I look at it every day.
LOUIS:	That fucking Pulitzer took pride of place on the mantelpiece of every place we ever lived.
BOA:	I married you.

LOUIS:	It was the first thing you'd show people: it even has a little coaster that it sits on/
BOA:	I'm proud of you.
LOUIS:	A little coaster suddenly appeared under it one day.
BOA:	I loved you.
LOUIS:	I mean eventually, after a week in bed, with a ballerina(!) –
BOA:	Oh stop it!
LOUIS:	I bet you can still put your legs behind your head/
BOA:	Louis!
LOUIS:	We fetishized each other! That's what worked!
BOA:	Not always! Back-fired a few times!
LOUIS:	After a week I staggered down to the ripped-out kitchen. I stood in the shell of it.
BOA:	What are you thinking?
LOUIS:	I gotta keep this place.
BOA:	Good.
LOUIS:	Boa, you know I'm on the road a lot.
BOA:	I know.
LOUIS:	Come live in the Bowery with me?
BOA:	Live with you?
LOUIS:	Yeah. You have to live with me forever.
BOA:	Is this some sort of proposal?

LOUIS:	Yeah I think it is.
BOA:	Because you'll have to get past my Mother.
LOUIS:	I can do that.
BOA:	You'd better get on your knees then.
LOUIS:	Mm-mm! And down I went! A smitten young fool.
BOA:	I didn't want a marriage that was some sort of long, quiet walk to the grave, no! Yes we argued.
LOUIS:	Constantly!
BOA:	Because I always felt we were two people who had somehow managed the beautiful trick of remaining autonomous within a relationship. Because we're so oppositional. And yes, you're the most intellectually combative person I've ever met/
LOUIS:	And you're the most contrary/woman
BOA:	But I'm enormously proud that we each achieved, career-wise, things to be proud of. We did. But look at us, we survived, we've done all right for ourselves. Despite –

4.

BOA:	Can I ring you this time?
LOUIS:	I'll call every chance I get/
BOA:	Not at the hotel?

LOUIS: I'm only there when I arrive/ I don't

BOA: You need more socks than that, surely.
Oh god, please stay!

LOUIS: Please / not now

BOA: My last ever ballet!

LOUIS: I know! I wish I could be here!

BOA: I'm officially modern.

LOUIS: You said they'll tape it?

BOA: Yeah.

LOUIS: I want to be there for every show, I do!

BOA: I'm not trying to make you feel guilty.

LOUIS: I know.

BOA: But I've only just gotten over the last trip.
Passport?

LOUIS: Check.

BOA: I think you have an addiction to danger.

LOUIS: That's why I married *you*/

BOA: Oh well, at least I look good in black/

LOUIS: Oh stop!

BOA: The young widow! All right for
you, you're not the one left behind
wondering/ if you've made it/

LOUIS: Quit it.

BOA: I get so scared!

LOUIS: Love, sincerely, half the time we're shut up
in hotels, or I get taken on wild goose chases,
the most danger I'm in is eating airline food.

BOA:	There's plenty of news in this country!
LOUIS:	I gotta go.
BOA:	Is it guilt at a high draft number?
LOUIS:	What?
BOA:	And losing your mum and dad? Is there anything I should be doing to make you feel like life and safety are worthwhile?
LOUIS:	Don't level guilt at me, sweetheart. You didn't know me then/
BOA:	No, and I'm glad!
LOUIS:	Meaning?
BOA:	You were even more gun-ho!
LOUIS:	*Gung* ho!
BOA:	Ughh, gung-ho/
LOUIS:	You even know what you're saying?
BOA:	Yes I think you're reckless, and a danger junkie/
LOUIS:	Danger junkie!
BOA:	You don't stop to think how it feels here/
LOUIS:	You figured that war was some kinda game?
BOA:	You chose to go, and you still choose/
LOUIS:	I chose to go? I chose to go as a reporter!
BOA:	Of course, and that was noble/
LOUIS:	Our presence there…pressured Congress enough – Noble?!

BOA: But you were a teenager…and there *was* guilt, at being alive/

LOUIS: I am not a child! I'm not a little kid, Boa! Dicing with death outta some…Jesus! I don't see myself as reckless. I wouldn't begin to… I wouldn't have the nerve! You don't know the half of it…you know what? D'you know what happened at my draft board physical? The draft clerk, Mrs O'Reilly, is telling me all about her sons as she's checking me over. And finally she looks up, exasperated, from my form and says: 'But dear, isn't there anything *wrong* with you?' And I didn't have the nerve to fabricate…so I stay silent. I'm stood there, eighteen, completely terrified. I didn't think much beyond that… I remember thinking 'well at least Dad taught me to use a firearm.' She goes back through my form. 'Aha! Eczema! Do you take any medication for it?' And Finally I squeak: 'Ah, well… I put this cream on, and I've had a few UV treatments…but it's only on my arms, and it comes and it goes.' 'Oh well then, dear. You'd have trouble wearing those scratchy uniforms!' And I'm just blinking at Mrs O'Reilly. The kindly Irish angel. And she writes it all down and says 'Just bring me a letter from your physician.' So I got a physical deferment even though I was too terrified to fake one! That's how reckless I am! We all shoulda been more scared than we were…god knows what would've happened to me otherwise. So yeah. Maybe Mrs O'Reilly's kindness is what radicalized me. Something made me set on going to that war to *report* rather

20

than jumping to Canada. But reckless?
No! Recklessness is a term I save for the
governments of the world. All I know is
other boys in my class weren't coming
home. Nineteen was the average age they
were dying out there. Nineteen! And I
thought, I gotta stay alive to get the story
home. Look I've gotta go. The truth is,
Boa. You make me want to live, very
much. Ok? You and Mrs O'Reilly are my
guardian angels. So I'll do my best.

BOA: I'm not much of guardian angel if I let
              you go.

LOUIS: I'll call. I love you so much.

BOA: Send me psychic messages too.

LOUIS: I will. Every day.

BOA: What's this?

LOUIS: S'you're opening night card.

BOA: Fuck!

LOUIS: Don't open it yet. I gotta go – break a leg.

5.

BOA: So while you were on assignment I
              kept the cocktail tradition alive in our
              little salon in The Bowery. Always
              had our friends drop by for gimlets
              and kamikazes, screwdrivers and long
              island iced teas from afternoon on. It all
              made boozing acceptable. Having my

little parties to stave off your looming disappointment with the world and my terrible loneliness. And the fear that you/

LOUIS: I liked getting home to a crowd, you hosting.

BOA: Americans are adorable drinkers!

LOUIS: But one day... I got home early. And you were so drunk, you were saturated, you stank.

Boa?

BOA: In here!

She doesn't get up.

LOUIS: Woah! Where's the party?

BOA: I can't dance.

LOUIS: Says who?

BOA: I won't dance again. The doctors, the physio.

LOUIS: We'll prove them wrong.

BOA: It was the fall.

LOUIS: Fall? He *dropped* you. That son of a bitch!

BOA: It's a dangerous sport.

(He points to her left shoulder.)

LOUIS: You said the clicking has stopped.

BOA: I know what I said.

LOUIS: You said it was better.

BOA: I say that so that you'll stop worrying but I'm in pain.

LOUIS:	It's that bad?
BOA:	How bad is bad?
LOUIS:	But – then what do we do?
BOA:	Louis dancers live in pain!
LOUIS:	I know, I know. Let's get you to bed.
BOA:	I thought I *was* in bed. This isn't my toenails flying off/
LOUIS:	I know!
BOA:	Our bodies resonate with it -
LOUIS:	I know, you have an astounding pain threshold.
BOA:	It's something you never get, about me/
LOUIS:	I do! You adapted to pain! You're incredible!
BOA:	But there's only so much adaptation I can do/
LOUIS:	I'm saying I get it, I do –
BOA:	Knees, hips, toe, achilles, I could deal with – but now the shoulder?
LOUIS:	All the time?
BOA:	Constant! Continuous!
LOUIS:	On a scale of?
BOA:	Oh Louis!
LOUIS:	Then we have to get it fixed, see every specialist! Every one!
BOA:	It's not going to mend, Louis. It's not just weight-bearing. They all say it's permanently weakened and liable to pop,

or tear. I feel it in extension. I'm done.
I'm retiring.

LOUIS: Maybe you could dance without your
shoulder. Lots of *(He demonstrates a dance
where his left shoulder remains unmoving.)*
and a bit of *(He struggles to dance and flails
about, mocking some contemporary dance
moves, nearly hurting himself, she laughs.)*

BOA: It's not funny.

LOUIS: No it's not funny. But drowning your
sorrows isn't gonna help. I don't want
you drinking alone.

BOA: Everyone drinks alone.

LOUIS: I mean the pair of us. We're alcoholics,
Boa.

BOA: No we're not!

LOUIS: Just because we don't start 'til after lunch
doesn't mean we're not reliant!

BOA: We are not dependent on booze!

LOUIS: You try walking in a straight line – now.

BOA: Oh goody-two-shoes here can hold his
liquor. It's a quality I find most charming
in a man!

LOUIS: You found it sexy. Hardened journalists
are supposed to drink.

BOA: Sexy? You drank like our parent's
generation. Staring into the glass,
drinking in bitter disappointment, with
the human race. With all of us. Because
sometimes, I felt your disappointment
with me too.

LOUIS:	Never! You grew so lonely. I disappointed you.
BOA:	No.
LOUIS:	I did. You wanted me home and then when I thought about quitting… everything changed. Suddenly we were both entering this early retirement and –

6.

BOA:	But you have the guts of a journalist. The instinct!
LOUIS:	Guts? I don't have guts!
BOA:	What do you mean?
LOUIS:	I don't know.
BOA:	Louis communicate, for god's sake!
LOUIS:	I don't know. Maybe I'm tired. You have no idea what it's like!
BOA:	Yes because you won't tell me! You call me and you want to hear about my dance classes, you come home and you want to go out and when I press you, you just say 'Oh, read the article' – when I want to know what your experience was. You know, tell me about Phnom Penh now!
LOUIS:	No!
BOA:	What's the difference if I'm going to read about it?

LOUIS:	I want to put it in a box. I want to come home and put it in a fucking box in the bottom of the closet! I want just once, not to have to talk about it.
BOA:	You never talk about it!
LOUIS:	And? Can't you respect that?
BOA:	No!
LOUIS:	Can't you respect that I sometimes really like to shove things away because that's maybe how *I* deal with them? That's how I process things Boa, I put them in a fucking box in my mind. I've got compartments!
BOA:	Where you lock things and throw away the key. It's unnerving... It's repression!
LOUIS:	It's better than just spilling everywhere!
BOA:	I spill?
LOUIS:	I'm sorry.
BOA:	I spill?
LOUIS:	Yeah...you *over*spill.
BOA:	Oh I'm sorry – am I a liquid mess you have to cope with? Well at least I feel something!
LOUIS:	Just because I don't scream and shout doesn't mean I don't feel something.
BOA:	It's not healthy, all the pent-up, buttoned-up – repressed/
LOUIS:	Well, it's me. It's how *I* deal. It's how *I* cope. Un-dramatic.
BOA:	You're telling *me*.

LOUIS:	If we both let loose we'd never get anything done!
BOA:	But… I feel excluded from your big grown-up world of war.
LOUIS:	Well, I'm sorry for that.
BOA:	It's a big impenetrable boy's club.
LOUIS:	*(Fuming.)* It's not a boy's club: there are plenty of women writers.
BOA:	Oh, I haven't met them! Where are you hiding them?
LOUIS:	Why do you do this? Why do you pick a fight? Just to get the reassurance at the end of it? I don't know. You keep going down this road and I'll lose my shit. If you want to see it, I'll lose it.
BOA:	One day someone will come and pull the lids off all your boxes. I just wish you'd let it out, a bit –
LOUIS:	If you feel excluded from my work that's *because* it's hard work…and it's punishing…but what would you know?
BOA:	There. Because I'm the spoilt brat who hasn't seen suffering first hand?
LOUIS:	Well Jesus Boa – maybe yeah – you act like it's a juicy story you're missing out on, but it's real people!
BOA:	Oh *I'm* the voyeur, am I?
LOUIS:	What does that mean?
BOA:	Yes, I'm drawn to people's suffering, it makes me feel! I don't think it's sinister/

27

LOUIS:	But now I've disappointed you. You married the hard-bitten war correspondent/
BOA:	I married you for your occupation?
LOUIS:	No. Well, maybe/
BOA:	Wow!
LOUIS:	The prestige?
BOA:	This is what you think of me?
LOUIS:	I think I/
BOA:	Wow, wow, wow. I think you'd better leave, Louis.
LOUIS:	No.
BOA:	Then I will.
LOUIS:	No you won't.
BOA:	Wanna bet? I take your goading, your mocking me, I take the insults about my supposed effing privilege and my ridiculous twirly life.
LOUIS:	No one on earth takes Spandex seriously!
BOA:	No – be honest! You think I'm with you for the glamour? Don't make me laugh! When you come back I swear…you have less light in your eyes. And if you think I fetishize that…you can just pack up and piss off. And stay gone.
LOUIS:	I can't.

She takes a long drink.

BOA:	Trauma doesn't look glam on someone you love, Louis. And I *know* you barely sleep. I can feel you awake in the night.
LOUIS:	I didn't know.
BOA:	Muttering syllables. Names, I think –
LOUIS:	I don't mean to wake you.
BOA:	I love the shit and the piss of you, Louis. Fuck journalism. I love you, especially. I don't know why, but I am indifferent to all other people because of you, you daft...prick. Your eyes, Louis. Your hands. Your disgusting habits. Your laugh. Your voice. You in all your youness. I love you in all your particularity. I love you like a parent loves their baby.
LOUIS:	Now that's a little creepy.
BOA:	*Your* hands. *Your* feet.
LOUIS:	Hello, Freud!
BOA:	No, fuck off! It's true. And please stop hurling Freud at me! It just makes you sound even more like a/
LOUIS AND BOA:	Smug Yankee Fuck.
BOA:	I've got no time for men who pathologise women/
LOUIS:	A simple 'I love you' would do.
BOA:	Come here.
LOUIS:	That – sometimes strangulating – love saved my life. And what a delicious mirror, hmm? To be seen to be special, by a woman like you. You did save my life, Boa. Over and over.

BOA:	Ha! Well I should get a Pulitzer! For studying the slow, slow...gradual impact of war and famine – on you.
LOUIS:	You might have thought it was slow but for me it was instantaneous.
BOA:	I was wrong to keep trying to *force* you to talk. You wouldn't talk. And then it came as a shock/
LOUIS:	I took refuge –
BOA:	In newpaper archives?
LOUIS:	It's a job.
BOA:	In the bottom of the New York Public Library? Literally under ground!
LOUIS:	I'm quitting for our health.
BOA:	You're a writer! How can you go from chasing the now to sitting there looking through mid-century microfilm?
LOUIS:	I took refuge in the past, Boa. I needed a hiatus from news. From the present, perhaps. Because my own drinking, though comparatively moderate, was to forget.
BOA:	I had married a haunted man.
LOUIS:	Yes, well, and – this wasn't resignation, this wasn't deciding to let injustices ride... I just wanted to take some time...to find... I thought about being a Thoreau scholar, remember?
BOA:	Do a Master's then, don't just disappear!
LOUIS:	Electronic news archives. You don't just preserve print journalism. You preserve a complete *picture* of the world at the time– you read a local paper from 1855, say/

BOA: 1855?

LOUIS: And you see the refugee districts springing up, you see cholera spreading from the slums; stamp duty abolished to make the news affordable, the advent of gossip columns and interviews – you see – you of course find this terminally boring.

BOA: You project that onto me. I just don't understand how you can stop writing! You love writing! Of course I want you safe at a desk but it's not you! Why, suddenly?

LOUIS: I'm getting old/

BOA: It's for me isn't it.

Beat.

Oh Christ... It's to keep an eye on me?

LOUIS: No, no/

BOA: What have I done?

LOUIS: In New York we were part of this grand, sparkling set of shiny people, Boa. Shiny impoverished artists on your side, shiny intellectuals and hacks on my side. I was no longer the dinner party darling. I got away from that world on purpose: it was all very purposeful.

He drinks.

LOUIS: Is that where I went wrong? Losing my nerve? Or not being plain-old cool enough?

BOA: Is that why you've come here? The blame game?

LOUIS: No.

BOA: Because I can go on all night, remember!

            You can't fix the past, Louis.

LOUIS: Yeah but – I think this is when I lost you.
            Our premature retirements.

BOA: Oh dear Louis! Always needing to
            pinpoint everything!

7.

LOUIS: It was at that point that I really lost you/

BOA: Well it wasn't quite the cabin in the
            woods you wanted/

LOUIS: At that moment you, my beloved girl,
            were launched into a pit of despair.

BOA: I always had black moods, you knew
            that/

LOUIS: Yeah but your…depression…was fuelled
            by continuing to stand in the wings
            watching the other dancers.

BOA: You had married a haunted woman.

LOUIS: Haunted by what?

BOA: Dunno – whatever caused me to spend
            my whole damned life in painful daily
            training! An obsessive and stubborn
            mindset, from childhood, my great
            escape, my singular passion –

LOUIS:	For christ's sake stop going to the theatre, stop watching them!
BOA:	I can't.
LOUIS:	Should I ban you from going?
BOA:	No.
LOUIS:	Then what?
BOA:	It's OK to just watch!
LOUIS:	You're torturing yourself!
BOA:	But it isn't about the other dancers! I watch them dance and somewhere in my brain I'm dancing too – they've discovered these things called mirror neurons and they say when we watch dance we're dancing too, inside, in the neural pathways...and I truly am! I don't need to block dance altogether!
	Jesus Christ I had to fight my way up! It was my whole life, Louis! First I was too tall for ballet – pointe shoes add three extra bloody inches – and now my dodgy shoulder! Fuck you Anna Pavlova and all you petite, you diminutive...you lucky little...short arses! Anatomy is destiny in ballet – but bloody hell! I just felt the injustice of it all, and I know worse things happen at sea but I genuinely felt my life was over. Louis... Incidentally it has never mended and if I throw it out of its socket it makes a little gristly sucking noise/
LOUIS:	Stop – I can't stand it! I always hated it when you did that!

BOA: You're squeamish about it. No… If it pops out it's hard to pop back in. Most of the time it's fine.

You were right about my depression. I was angry. But it wasn't just the dancing. Sometimes I felt like my anger belonged to another person, another time. I was a baby, a baby. We were babies then! Still growing! And I didn't now how to go on if I couldn't dance. I needed numb. But you always conflated depression and drinking, you needed to blame the external, blame the bottle.

LOUIS: You are going to drink yourself to death!

BOA: I'm a happy drunk, I'm not hurting anyone! Nobody minds – look –

LOUIS: Keep your voice down!

BOA: They should've put you in charge when thingy left!

LOUIS: Burt. And he's right behind you.

BOA: When *Burt* left!

LOUIS: I'm not qualified.

BOA: Absolute disregard for all your hard work!

LOUIS: My darling, I'm not a librarian!

BOA: You've gone blind! Setting up this database thingy!

LOUIS: Boa –

BOA: I should never have come to this sodding party. *(To the work party.)* Good evening Elmer, or Kyle, or Zach, or Clyde or

	Marshall, or Buzz or Dirk or Dick Head or whatever your funny American name is!
LOUIS:	These are my colleagues!
BOA:	But why are we underground with these people? You don't even want to be here, *(Loud.)* you've done more than they'll ever know!
LOUIS:	Control yourself.
BOA:	Control? You've thrown your career down the loo to work with a bunch of cardigan-wearing archivists, now you're content to be a has-been: why? Because you've lost your nerve! Oh no, sorry, because of me!
LOUIS:	Get a hold of yourself!
BOA:	Hear that everyone, I am officially out of control! I am a wild, madwoman and I need curtailing!

8.

LOUIS:	Oh god, don't remind me.
BOA:	That night.
LOUIS:	You'd had a bit to drink. We were just a bunch of academics, yet somehow you felt judged – more than you ever had around journalists.
BOA:	I don't remember the rest.

LOUIS:	Lucky you!
BOA:	I didn't feel judged.
LOUIS:	Well you sure felt something!
BOA:	But, that night was the real reason we moved back to England, wasn't it? Shit.
LOUIS:	They weren't going to forget that little speech in a hurry.
LOUIS:	You have humiliated yourself tonight.
BOA:	Nobody cares! Nobody cares about you half as much as you think! You get so wound up when really, no one's bothered if you've got a drunk wife with a loose tongue!
LOUIS:	I'm just beginning to understand that fine line they say between love, and hate.
BOA:	Oh, no, have I just crossed it? Divorce me then you shrewish little man!
LOUIS:	Drink some water.
BOA:	No? You can't?! You can't bear to leave me. You are nothing without me.
LOUIS:	Keep telling yourself that Boa!
BOA:	Go fuck yourself.
LOUIS:	Worst thing is you won't remember this in the morning.
BOA:	Lucky I've got you to remind me of every terrible thing I've ever done.
LOUIS:	And I'll carry the shame of you all by myself.
BOA:	You're ashamed of me?

LOUIS:	Yeah! Sometimes I'm disgusted by you.
BOA:	That's because I'm disgusting! Well… If I'm so…fucking disgusting then I'll go, shall I? Leave you in peace once and for all!
LOUIS:	Where you going, you're butt naked –
BOA:	Anywhere that's not here.
LOUIS:	Don't be silly. It's the middle of the night.
BOA:	Fuck off.
LOUIS:	Boa. I don't care. I don't give a fuck! Half of what you said tonight is true.
BOA:	You hate me, and I'm disgusting apparently!
LOUIS:	You're drunk.
BOA:	Either you get out or I go!
LOUIS:	You cannot throw our relationship against the wall every time we argue! It's not fair!
BOA:	I don't want to throw us against the wall I want to throw me against the wall, I want to smash my brain in, I want to not think! Sometimes I just want to stop…having thoughts to stop being – to stop this whir, whir, whir of fucking –
LOUIS:	No! No. Listen. You cannot threaten to leave – or kick me out – during every argument. You cannot end our marriage during every fight. You can't. You cannot.
BOA:	Don't patronise me/
LOUIS:	I can't live like this any more! I can't! It's just…untenable…! I cannot actually live…like this…any more!

BOA: Then leave!

LOUIS: Aghhhh! See?! This is exactly what I just asked you not to do.

BOA: If you don't like it, leave.

LOUIS: Grow up.

BOA: I dare you to leave.

LOUIS: Maybe I should!

BOA: Get the fuck out then and never come back.

LOUIS: You're dragging me down with you! I just want you to be happy! I just want you… to be happy.

BOA: I can't stand being around you any longer.

LOUIS: No. You know what you can't stand? What you can't stand is being loved by me! What you cannot fucking *bear* is being loved! Because you *hate* yourself! You hate yourself, you stupid fucking idiot! I wish you saw you as I do but you don't, and that my darling is our problem, your fucking self esteem! So you can blame me all you like for you feeling small…but the real problem…the real *problem*… Is that you think anyone who loves you is a fucking idiot! And… and… I'm tired of you saying I 'make' you feel like this, or I 'make' you feel like that. Nobody can *make* you feel anything you don't *want* to feel! Nobody can! If you had a modicum of self-esteem you might know that. God, I wish you knew that!

BOA:	I'm mad, I'm psychotic, I need to see a doctor.
LOUIS:	You talk so much shit about yourself I'm starting to believe it!
BOA:	Fuck you –
	(She begins to hyperventilate.)
LOUIS:	Boa, Boa, Boa. Calm down. Calm down.
BOA:	No…god, Louis… I don't think you're a coward!
LOUIS:	I know.
BOA:	You're my favourite person in the whole…world… God Louis, I think I'm a real…mess!
LOUIS:	You're not.
BOA:	I am. Don't you think I should be medicated? I humiliated you – I should just be put down! I'm no good for you. I'm no good for anyone! I'm not good. I'm not good. Oh god Louis, I'm not good –

9.

LOUIS:	I never knew what to say to you, that's when my words failed me. I shoulda been able to help you.
BOA:	How could you? Sometimes after those rows, Louis – I'd wake up in the morning

afraid I'd punched you. I felt, on waking, such remorse/

LOUIS: Well it's hard to get to the bottom of it… Nowadays I think… I mean depression *appears* soft and low and sad, and seems to have nothing to do with anger. On the *outside* that is. But we all know, don't we? It's fury. I think it's rage.

BOA: I disagree, I think it was fear. I think it's fear, with me. And maybe chemical.

LOUIS: I was always trying to manipulate you, wasn't I?

BOA: Were you?

LOUIS: I tried to make you think that moving to London was your idea.

10.

BOA: God maybe… I was just so thrilled to get you out of your little paper lair in the bottom of the library.

LOUIS: The day we land I'm hauled along to publicly mourn Princess Diana.

BOA: Mother had met her once at a hospice.

LOUIS: Yes! Now we're getting to it – your mother, Mary –

BOA: They say marry a man your Mother is half in love with!

LOUIS:	No. Marry a man who loves you more than you love him.
BOA:	My mother has to be restrained she's so in love with you!
LOUIS:	I'm living round the corner from my mother-in-law.
BOA:	It's rent-free!
LOUIS:	She pinches my ass!
BOA:	She does it to all the boys!
LOUIS:	I had hoped that you might turn some of your anger back towards your family, away from yourself. I was looking for the source. Your mother – still alive?
BOA:	Yep/
LOUIS:	I knew it! She'll go on forever! Your mother – so perfectly charming to everyone in the world except you. I was shocked Boa!
BOA:	I wanted you to hate her.
LOUIS:	I wanted you to stand up to her!
BOA:	She's all I have.
LOUIS:	You had me! You had me on your side. But you never tried, Boa. I got busy trying to earn money…giving journalism lectures without a doctorate. I felt – necessary again!
BOA:	Well who needs a measly PhD when you've seen Saigon fall! Ahh, see how they fawn over the world-weary American! Have you ever fucked your students?

LOUIS:	What?
BOA:	I used to smell death on you and now it's cheap perfume.
LOUIS:	Don't you dare.

11.

LOUIS:	See I don't know what you were doing while I was at work. You constructed fantasies of betrayal. Maybe because Mummy was right there.
BOA:	Mother is the hammer, we are the anvil!
LOUIS:	You lived there, in Little Venice, in our squalid flat, playing house in girlish delirium, going quietly mad – can I say that? You went mad. And you stopped being Boa, this warrior of a woman I had fallen in love with.
BOA:	You fell out of love.
LOUIS:	Not for a second! But you got...small! I'm sorry, you got small-minded! And I would come home, frustrated at the world,
BOA:	Because you never gave up *reading* the news/
LOUIS:	And you were drinking.
BOA:	Moderately, I had reined it in.
LOUIS:	But the fights!

BOA:	I know. Suddenly in England I was walking round in an apron, dishing out/
LOUIS:	You couldn't be *you* near that dark, over-stuffed, old house. I grew to hate it. That house sucked you back into the fifties.
BOA:	We did try with you, Louis! My family embraced you. I wanted to un-orphan you. But while you were drawn, curious, moth-like, to such a large brood – you were also repelled. Admit it! At any family gathering you would always find a place to hide.

12.

BOA:	Aha! There you are! Why are you hiding in here?
	LOUIS sees Hamilton Barksby.
LOUIS:	What the hell *is* that?
BOA:	What?
LOUIS:	That – skeleton?
BOA:	Oh it's my Dad's!
LOUIS:	What do you mean it's your Dad's?
BOA:	Father stole him from Medical School.
LOUIS:	I thought you meant –
	They laugh.
BOA:	No! That's Hamilton Barksby!

LOUIS:	And your fucking brothers would leave this wired skeleton dangling from the rafters just to scare the shit out of me! One minute, Hamilton Barksby would be lazing on the stairs...the next, he'd be suspended from a lampshade or spread-eagled in the hall in a dress and trilby. And none of you seemed to mind...the irony...that the one reminder of your Dad was a dead thing, hung over all of your lives.
LOUIS:	It's wearing my pyjama pants!
BOA:	Do you hate them? My family?
LOUIS:	Noooo, I don't *hate* them!
BOA:	But?
LOUIS:	But are you happy in England? Playing house?
BOA:	Well it's all right for you – you've still got passions. And you're fundamentally happy.
LOUIS:	That's not true. I have my moments.
BOA:	Well OK, but – you default happy, I default sad. I might leap about and be hyper, but inside? I'm a bleak, melancholic waste of space.
LOUIS:	Ohh woe is Boa! Poor Boa!
BOA:	They did tell me at school I had a sunny disposition.
	They giggle.
LOUIS:	So what went wrong?
	They giggle.

BOA: Is that what you want even now, Louis? Still frustrated by a lack of evidence? Well, eventually I got a therapist and I unpacked my childhood. I punched a pillow pretending it was my Mother's face and still, still – the responsibility lies with me, Louis. I have to believe the brain is plastic. Because I did, I let go of things. I shed something. I've changed.

LOUIS: Good. I never really thought it was chemical.

BOA: Then I'm just a sad person! Can't I just be sad?! I'm sorry. But look at the world Louis, I have every reason to be sad.

LOUIS: But we're so fucking FORTUNATE!

BOA: – Exactly.

LOUIS: Well who asked you to be despondent on behalf of humankind?

13.

BOA: But martyrs are so attractive! I mean look at you on campus. You're a hero. A martyr of all the world's pain! And what've you got waiting for you at home? Just a flimsy, gin-soaked idiot.

LOUIS: I do not want to fuck my students, Boa! I pity them, thinking they can still be cub reporters – I should burst their bubble! But I like being surrounded by hope. Baby socialists dreaming dreams, it feels hopeful! It may even be sexy. But

	I can assure you, I'm some sorta ancient mentor figure in their eyes!
BOA:	That must be very frustrating!
LOUIS:	I am *not* interested in screwing around, with teenagers or with anybody. But I might as well have!
BOA:	Might as well what?
LOUIS:	Ohhh I don't know! All the accusations, all the time! I might as well have had an affair if I'm going to be punished for one!
BOA:	I can feel it. I've got good instincts.
LOUIS:	I don't wanna tell you you're imagining things, but you really need to stop this. Have I ever given you reason to think/
BOA:	Did you fuck someone else when you were away? In Chile, maybe? That fortnight without contact?
LOUIS:	I could map…my trips around the globe by all the treks in search of working payphones to call you. I spent so much of my time hunting for phones that I didn't have the time for all my affairs!
BOA:	That's not true.
LOUIS:	It's not true. No.
BOA:	What?
LOUIS:	I mean the thought was there…yes.
BOA:	I know you didn't.
LOUIS:	Yes from time to time I was in a hotel overseas and I didn't know when I was coming home, I was seeing the worst

	humanity has to offer and sometimes yes, there's a woman in the bar in the hotel/
BOA:	Well I'd never have known!
LOUIS:	And I'd think sometimes… I could probably get laid if I played my cards right! But I didn't. I didn't! I never have! But thank you, for yet again questioning my love, my moral scruples, and my self-respect.
BOA:	Oh your 'scruples' are above questioning!
LOUIS:	Did you? With one of the straight dancers?
BOA:	I could have.
LOUIS:	I know! They're a damn sight more attractive than my cronies!
BOA:	No, Louis. I didn't.
LOUIS:	You sure? Because put a bunch of you in a rehearsal room for a month and the passions doth arise!
	(They laugh.)
BOA:	I'm sorry.
LOUIS:	Where does this *come* from?
BOA:	I don't know.
LOUIS:	I get attacked the minute I walk through the door!
BOA:	I build it up in my head all day/
LOUIS:	Do I trigger it, somehow?
BOA:	No. It's something in the set-up… I mean, look at us!

LOUIS:	What?
BOA:	It's like the nineteen bloody fifties!
LOUIS:	You're being suffocated.
BOA:	It's not your fault.
LOUIS:	'Cause I don't want that!
BOA:	Neither do I!
LOUIS:	I never asked you to wash my underwear! I kinda like washing yours!
BOA:	I know!
LOUIS:	It's not me…wanting this.
BOA:	I know. But I'm frightened I enjoy it! I'm frightened I'm growing contented by you as bread-winner and me as pant-washer and I'm disappearing into some old, ancient regime…content to live the life of a flower… *(He laughs.)* and I'll curl up in a ball and…become some sort of foul-mouthed imitation of my Mum – *(They laugh.)*
	– when all I really want to do is punch!
LOUIS:	Uh oh!
BOA:	Not you – life. I mean I want to *fight*, but I've lost my – fight –
LOUIS:	Then do something!
BOA:	I'm no good at anything!
LOUIS:	You're not good at one single thing, you can do everything!
BOA:	I can't play piano or fly planes.

LOUIS:	Then learn. Nature didn't adapt us to fly planes or play piano, we taught ourselves.
BOA:	Uhhh balls to your quasi-religious notion of nature!
LOUIS:	This is equality Boa, this is the secret women are party to now!
BOA:	Oh balls to your pseudo-feminism!
LOUIS:	Call it training then/
BOA:	All my body knows is dancing.
LOUIS:	Train yourself, to do something else that you love.
BOA:	All right. OK. You know what? I will.
LOUIS:	What?
BOA:	I will. For you… I shall cut a new path!
BOA:	I decided to learn ceramics, fancied myself as a potter. I did, didn't I? I learned ceramics?

She presents a large vase to him.

LOUIS:	It's very lovely.
BOA:	You don't think it looks/
LOUIS:	Like a…/
BOA:	What?
LOUIS:	Like…no go on: you say?
BOA:	Like a cock?
LOUIS:	No!
BOA:	It does.
LOUIS:	Maybe if you paint it/

BOA: Oh sod it!

LOUIS: We had these beautiful moments of clarity...of...sobriety.

BOA: Then I got so drunk at that baptism that I started a fight with my cousins.

LOUIS: A physical fight, smirking at other's people's faith.

BOA: That's when you and my Mother really had to be in cahoots.

LOUIS: We threatened rehab.

BOA: All I needed was a therapist. Who knew AA was so insufferably Christian, I wasn't going there!

14.

BOA: *(Drunk.)* Well! I thought that was a lovely supper.

LOUIS: Let's get you to bed.

BOA: No.

LOUIS: See when was the last time you had to take my pants off me, hey?

BOA: I always –

LOUIS: When was the last time you had to undress me?

BOA: If you died, then I'd go out and fuck about.

LOUIS: So would I. I'd screw anything I could. Men and women.

BOA:	Good lad.
LOUIS:	Then I'd fall to pieces.
BOA:	Then I'd kill myself.
LOUIS:	You would not.
BOA:	I would. I wouldn't know how to be any more.
LOUIS:	Don't I can't even think about it.
BOA:	Oh surely you do! I fantasise about you dying all the time!
LOUIS:	How'm I dying then?
BOA:	Dunno. Drowning in a sea of your own bilious pomposity...or stepping into an empty elevator shaft or...bitten by a butterfly...with rabies...or you get sucked down a plug hole.
LOUIS:	*(Sings.)*
	'My baby has gone down the plug-hole,
BOA	*(Joins.)* My baby has gone down the plug;
	Poor little thing
	Was so skinny and thin:
	Shoulda been washed in a jug! In a jug!
	My baby is perfectly happy,
	He won't need a bath any more;
	He's a-mucking about
	With the angels above:
	Not lost, but gone on before!'
BOA:	A voice like an angel!

LOUIS:	Thank you darling/
BOA:	What comes after death?
LOUIS:	Nothing. I think.
BOA:	Me too. I find it comforting. Otherwise we'd squander what time we have.
LOUIS:	Says the heavyweight boozer.
BOA:	Oh shush.
LOUIS:	I'd go in for some reincarnation.
BOA:	You're coming back as a dung beetle.
LOUIS:	You ever see the ourobouros on a tombstone?
BOA:	The northern lights?
	(They laugh.)
LOUIS:	No…ourobouros/
BOA:	Ourobouros/
LOUIS:	A circular snake, eating its tail. Symbolises the eternal return.
BOA:	You should get that tattooed.
LOUIS:	Endless. Like us.
BOA:	Louis, is there a difference between inexplicable and unexplainable?
LOUIS:	Ah, now there is! In my opinion! Do you want to hear it?
BOA:	No. I want a baby.
LOUIS:	OK, that's sobering! Er…you never have before.

BOA:	I want to have a part of you with me when you're not here.
LOUIS:	That's not a good enough reason.
BOA:	No.
LOUIS:	I think that's a terrible reason.
BOA:	Don't you want my children?
LOUIS:	Want them? Now?
BOA:	Yes.
LOUIS:	Isn't it dangerous?
BOA:	Maybe.
LOUIS:	If you're serious about this then we'll discuss. In the morning.
BOA:	I'm too old. I've gone off.
LOUIS:	Could you stay sober for nine months? Could you stay sober afterwards?
BOA:	What?
LOUIS:	It's a serious question. Or there's adoption/
BOA:	Oh well you'd have to retire – again – to make sure I didn't drop the fucking baby!
LOUIS:	You didn't want one when you were dancing, and now you want one?
BOA:	Yes! And now you don't?
LOUIS:	Your light was red – for years, your light was red when mine was green!
BOA:	And now?
LOUIS:	I don't know.

BOA: What does that mean? What does that mean your light *was* green? Now your light is red?'

LOUIS: I'm not sure... I'd have to think about it/

BOA: No you fucking won't, tell me now/

LOUIS: *(Erupts.)* Boa I'd have to think about it!

BOA: You don't want to have children with me?

LOUIS: No!

BOA: No?

LOUIS: I don't know!

BOA: You don't want a family?

LOUIS: I don't know. I don't know! Do I have to respond to your every damn whim on the spot?

BOA: Yes!

LOUIS: You want me to answer right now?

BOA: Yes!

LOUIS: Right now the answer is no.

BOA: No children.

LOUIS: Yes: no.

BOA: You don't want to have my children?

LOUIS: That's not what I'm saying/

BOA: My kids specifically, or generally/

LOUIS: Generally, not yours – or anyone else's/

BOA: Who else's would you have?

LOUIS: Boa, seriously/

BOA:	We're not having a family?
LOUIS:	No.
BOA:	Because you say so?
LOUIS:	It's fifty percent my decision and I'd say, judging by how many units you manage to put away each week, no, we are not fit to be parents.
BOA:	I'd stop.
LOUIS:	Please! Please do! Please give it a go and then we'll have this conversation some other time/
BOA:	Fuck you/
LOUIS:	When you've succeeded/
BOA:	Massive fuck you. You don't get to tell me what I can do with my body, my womb. You don't get to decide this Louis! You don't get to say 'No' to my body, to my biological imperative!
LOUIS:	You don't want children!
BOA:	And now, now when I want them you would deny me/
LOUIS:	Now? Right now? Right now I don't think I'd want you in the same room as my children!
	Pause.
BOA:	That is…unforgiveable.
LOUIS:	Is it?
BOA:	Louis –

LOUIS:	Don't erupt… Boa… I can't see how we'd make it work… I don't even really…like to be around kids, is the truth…since/
BOA:	But you're brilliant with kids!
LOUIS:	When I started out in Cambodia…two days in, in fact…I thought after 'Nam I could take anything but the opposite in fact, see I wasn't hardened to it, I was maybe more broken-hearted than ever… Boa…they pulled the body of a teacher out of the Mekong…and he had, strapped to him…a child tied to each limb, they had weighted him down…but he looked like a big, messy starfish…his pupils –

15.

BOA:	Thank you.
	(Beat.)
	My therapist says you need a therapist.
LOUIS:	Let me guess, she recommends a friend.
BOA:	You're haunted so badly we can't have children, and you won't take any action at all.
LOUIS:	I don't think we'd be fit parents is why I don't want children!
BOA:	I know I'm overly dramatic but I don't think I can bear another year of living with your locked up boxes.

LOUIS:	Well I can't bear another year of watching you decay!
BOA:	That's horrible.
LOUIS:	What's horrible is a middle-aged drunk. Not so cute on you now.
BOA:	Because you deliberately said that to hurt me I'm going to struggle to forgive you.
LOUIS:	I'm sorry.
	All right!
BOA:	All right what?
LOUIS:	I want to go on a trip – back.
BOA:	Back where?
LOUIS:	Back there. East Asia.
BOA:	No you don't, do you? Said you could never go back.
LOUIS:	Maybe this is what I need. I couldn't stomach a head doctor, Boa.
BOA:	Then we'll plan it. I can help you plan it. You'll go back. Do you want to go alone?
LOUIS:	Would you come with me? Can you bear it?
BOA:	I'm coming. We'll go together.
LOUIS:	But can you bear it, Boa… If *I* struggle?
BOA:	Oh my darling. Yes. Yes I can.
	He drinks.
BOA:	Where did we start?
LOUIS:	Thailand for the millennium, and crossed into Cambodia.

16.

BOA:	I found a pharmacy! How're you doing?
LOUIS:	About a hundred pounds lighter.
BOA:	Electrolyte powders/
LOUIS:	Thanks/
BOA:	To hydrate you. And repellent. Put it on.

LOUIS jumps up.

LOUIS:	Go out on the balcony!
BOA:	Why?
LOUIS:	The walls are paper-thin!

He exits to the toilet at a pace.

BOA:	Which end's it coming out of?
LOUIS:	*(Off.)* Shut up! I've no dignity left!

She sings the chorus of Phil Och's 'Draft Dodger Rag':

'I'm only eighteen, I got a ruptured spleen,

And I always carry a purse;

(LOUIS joins in, from the bathroom.)

I got eyes like a bat, my feet are flat, and my asthma's gettin' worse;

Yes, think of my career, my sweetheart dear, and my poor old invalid aunt,

Besides I ain't no fool, I'm a-goin' to school

And I'm workin' in a DEE-fense plant.'

BOA: Have you been smoking?

LOUIS: *(Off.)* It was Heang, he came up/

BOA: You won't believe it, Louis, practically the first people I try to chat to are dancers!

LOUIS: *(off.)* You people are everywhere!

BOA: *(She swats a mosquito, misses it.)* My tuk tuk driver told me he was a child soldier. How he shot eight people, wants to show me a mass grave across town. He wasn't boasting, or, selling me a story, you know?

LOUIS: *(Off.)* Uhuh/

BOA: Tomorrow he's taking me to the next village. *(She swats a mosquito, misses it.)* Do you think you'll be well enough?

LOUIS: *(Off.)* I hope so! I better be!

BOA: I haven't seen a single old person.

He returns.

LOUIS: No.

She rubs his back.

BOA: How is Heang?

LOUIS: He seems very happy. He's a fisherman now; you know he's my age?

BOA: Is he?

LOUIS: I felt sure he was older. Speaks five languages.

BOA: Was he pleased to see you?

LOUIS:	Well he's invited us back to Koh Rong. He's built some bungalows. We just turn up.
BOA:	Was it strange, or sad, or?
LOUIS:	No we laughed! He found the stomach flu very amusing.
BOA:	But did you say we'd love to go, to the island?
LOUIS:	I said you already had it on the itinerary.
BOA:	Are you ok?
LOUIS:	Yeah. Tell me about these twirlies!
BOA:	Ok well… Soriya and Nakry – they've saved a lot of Khmer folk dance from wipe out…we've been in absolute hysterics, them teaching me…they met in a refugee camp on the Thai border… their families were killed. *(She swats a mosquito, gets it.)* Yes! And in the camp, as little girls, to…survive…they taught themselves the male parts of the dance from the empty-space memory of the missing boys. They're trying to keep minority dances alive. They would've been erased! Anyway I just about picked one up, I'll show you.
LOUIS:	God damn it.
BOA:	What?
LOUIS:	Nothing.
BOA:	What?
LOUIS:	God, Boa. Sometimes I – find it all in bad taste, okay?

BOA:	What's in bad taste?
LOUIS:	Your *enjoyment* –
BOA:	Of?
LOUIS:	Forgive me, I've been cooped up.
BOA:	You think I enjoy…what, exactly?
LOUIS:	Ignore me love. I've been going over things after Heang left. Enforced reflection, if you will.
BOA:	Do you think I find genocide erotic?
LOUIS:	Now woah! No! Who said that?
BOA:	It never changes. You're allowed to gravely report the world's misdemeanours, but if *I* go anywhere near them, oh! I'm a gleeful, privileged white girl.
LOUIS:	That's not at all what I'm saying, I'm tired, I'm not in my right mind today/
BOA:	I know how hard it is to come here again. I had *hoped* you be invigorated… I had *hoped* you'd observe the corruption, maybe write a few notes…But you attack *me*. Well let me tell you something once and for all, Louis. I don't have time for those who sneer about 'liberal guilt.' That's how the right-wingers make their excuses! And I know if I was a true liberal I wouldn't write all the Republicans and Tories off as uncompassionate… But here's where we differ about guilt… I cherish it! I think the world needs a conscience! Conscience expressed politically – that'd be my dream! I think it's good to be troubled

by hunger and poverty and limited political freedom. You can't have it both ways! Walk the walk before you call me a hypocrite, before you call me some sort of *leech* on other's suffering... I will no longer be ashamed of my compassion for others, of my spillage, of my fellow-feeling! I'm no fucking angel, Louis, and I'm not a useful humanitarian, but I feel responsibility, not just to the things that affect *me*. I am the first to say how lucky I am to have my place at the feast! But do you think it truly tastes good when I can see people starving as I chew?

LOUIS: Whaddya gonna do with this?

BOA: With this what?

LOUIS: Righteous anger.

BOA: Shove it up your arse.

LOUIS: I love you.

BOA: You're crying.

17.

BOA: And that's when *I* became necessary again. I began to *make* work. More of the kind you hate.

LOUIS: I don't hate it.

BOA: There *is* something sacred for me about dancing. Don't make that face. It's the energy you create, and share – I get to

collaborate with people in the world who
see dance – *(To LOUIS.)* and you can shut
up – as a kind of survival. The people
I've met!

LOUIS: I was about to buy you a dog, I read it
helps depression, to have to take care
of something. I was ready to get you to
Battersea to find you a mutt!

BOA: But in Cambodia I learnt to choreograph.
And you cried.

LOUIS: I did.

BOA: And I was strong.

LOUIS: And after all these years…you were
happy. We were happy. You were fucking
sober! All these years trying every damn
trick in the book and dance saved your
life! Your being at the barre – the right
kinda bar /

BOA: Ohh, very good/

LOUIS: Doing the thing that makes you happy
– this whole damn time you should'a
been choreographing! All that time you
shoulda been making, god help me,
'Blood and Honey'! I spent all these years
thinking about you, what I should be
doing, how I could… I moved our life
to London, to your insufferable brothers
and Hamilton fucking Barksby and your
damned mother, and you…made yourself
better.

BOA: Gosh sorry Louis did you want to be the
one that fixed me?

LOUIS: Yeah, I probably did.

Beat.

No. I needed you sick.

You could express your sadness. I couldn't. I maybe stayed strong for Dad. The pair of us kept a lid on it. I pretended to myself, to the world, even, that I was your caretaker but it was grandiose of me. I lived my sadness out through you/

BOA: You don't need to apologise

LOUIS: To explain, then/

BOA: It's too late for that Louis! We've said all this/

LOUIS: Please! In truth I needed to be beside you in your pain. When I couldn't ever express mine. I needed yours. I needed yours.

BOA: But I started drying out and my career took off!

LOUIS: You deserved it. I got to experience being the one left behind.

BOA: I was finally making money – being invited back to *direct* in New York was huge for me Louis!

LOUIS: I was so proud!

BOA: *You* had to come with *me!*

18.

LOUIS:	Boa. Here's what I have to tell you.
BOA:	Uh oh.
LOUIS:	Remember you had that rare edition of *Jane Eyre* with you?
BOA:	You said 'don't take that with you it'll get dog-eared.' Yes.
LOUIS:	You always travelled with your gloomy Yorkshire girls.
BOA:	Look, I know, I left it. In a bar in Siem Reap.
LOUIS:	I had it in my rucksack.
BOA:	You found it?
LOUIS:	Well, no…remember I still had stomach flu at the station and there was no restroom? Ahh… Boa, I – wiped my ass with *Jane Eyre*.
BOA:	You did what?
LOUIS:	I knew you would never forgive the impertinence, so I lied! And I blamed you.
BOA:	I don't believe it!
LOUIS:	I honestly did dither about whether to tear those pages out/
BOA:	Defecating on a book?
LOUIS:	Well technically, no, I was using the leaves to…look I couldn't walk back through the crowd of tourists to you… covered in shit. I mean, Boa, it was bad,

| | it was an explosive one, it was a black, Bacchic fountain of a shit/ |

BOA: God, stop!/

LOUIS: Liquid dark and pretty much unwipeable, I was a mess!

BOA: You let me think, all these years/

LOUIS: Ah, yes, but if you think about it you'd rather lose a second edition than see a grown man spattered with his own dung! Given that you still wouldn't let me piss when you were in the shower, I felt I had no choice!

BOA: I almost wish you hadn't told me!

LOUIS: I'm sorry. I thought it a good moment for confession.

BOA: You sacrificed a Brontë!

LOUIS: I did.

BOA: You've never told me this before?

LOUIS: I've always felt terrible about poor Jane!

BOA: No – no – no Louis. This is new information!

LOUIS: Is that so strange?

BOA: You can't tell me something new!

LOUIS: What?

BOA: I must be mad.

19.

BOA: I know you said we didn't merge, but we did. You're still bleeding into me! This beautiful force of Blood. Blood with all the force of its 'B'. 'Bbbh'.

When I danced… I always imagined we have concentric circles of compassion and it starts with blood. That wonderful affection which near relations are supposed to conceive for one another. Concentric circles, ripples of empathy, moving out from the centre. There's me in the middle with my self-interest. Then there's your family. Then your friends and lovers maybe, then colleagues and acquaintances, then strangers and passersby, out and out and out and out and out until the circle of people you've never met or will never meet. People who were in a different time and space to you. And people move between our circles, in the ripples, out and in, slow and fluid. But You now, you're – in another category all together –

LOUIS: I agree. It's confusing for us both… I hear what you're saying…/

BOA: No, no. For me to do this, to speak with you now – I have to say it any old way I can. I need you to just hear everything even if I'm talking nonsense now because I might be nuts and if I'm nuts –

LOUIS: OK. OK.

BOA: Because maybe this is the *when* I am speaking of: the passing of you into me. Listen – the *when* of it on that day. Watching bloodthreads worm about in your scotch-coloured piss bag.

Also earlier, on the day, I passed this redundant telephone box and one side was smashed in. Smashed out, rather – ice blue crunchy glass under foot, and in the middle of it, on the glass, what stopped me was one wing. A black wing. A single lost dead black wet lost dead thing –

LOUIS: Oh god.

20.

BOA: I need you to understand what it was like for me. You were lying on the hospital bed, like a little tree across the road, cut down....you looked so small Louis. Your shoulders this wide like a child's coat hanger......your whole body thin as a wisp like a piece of dry cleaning, like a heron rising, narrow –

LOUIS: Darling.

BOA: What? Yes?

LOUIS: Similes truly are the sarcophagus of an image.

BOA: Oh fuck off Louis!

LOUIS: I'm sorry.

BOA:	Thing is, you're not sorry! You're not, look at you!
LOUIS:	Please. Carry on. Please.
BOA:	OK. So I was sitting there, finally feeling the lethal effects of time. I need some air. I'm light-headed, and the air is thick. I go down to the quadrangle and sit on a bench. A few patients are out getting illicit suction from cigarettes. A woman in a pale blue dressing gown finishes her cigarette and sprays herself with a giant aerosol can and then puts it back in the gown pocket. I smell something alpine. Probably gone back in to hook herself up to a drip. All the while I'm thinking, I need a few minutes outside, but have you died up there? Looking up at your window. What tense are you? Past? Present? Now are you dead? Now? Now? Or now? Because part of you, part of me wants to not be there. When it comes, whatever it is – and my head races with 'who shall I phone first' as if, in some perverse way – I need the practicalities, but I can't grasp practicalities! I've really, I've just come out here – I have a good cry. A good fucking belter of a cry. Big wet sobs with a wet chin and tears in my mouth. But no one troubles you if you have a bit of a weep in hospital grounds. '*She's* lost someone' or '*She's* seen the worst' or '*She's* seen it comin, poor bitch'. And I am, I have, haven't I?

There's no getting away from you! You love me like a limpet!

LOUIS:	Like a barnacle. Like a mollusc on a whale, a flea on a dog, I love you like/
BOA:	Bouquets of flowers, cinched to a tree.
LOUIS:	What?

21.

BOA:	Do you remember at the beginning of us as a thing I would run into the oddest people?
LOUIS:	Of course.
BOA:	The man who forcibly read my aura on the South Bank, the guy in Washington Square!
LOUIS AND BOA	'This heat dried up my dick girl, this heat!'
	They laugh.
BOA:	You called me a Freak Magnet but I saw such beauty… In us all…some days we were both sort of aggHHHhhhhhh *Humanity!* You know?
LOUIS:	Aghhhhhh! Yep!
	They laugh.
BOA:	We're all just fucking crazy, aren't we?! We're all just lovely fucking fuck-ups, we're all of us – *completely* – mental!
LOUIS:	We're all fucking whackjobs!! Yes!
BOA:	And anyway your dying – well Jesus – what the fuck *was* that? See it wasn't

filmic, or dramatic, sudden or anything,
it was rubbish. How did *you* not go out
with a bang? In fact, your dying was sort
of only marked by your being absent, or
stopped – by – your not– and in truth
I couldn't be exact because there's the
formal checking, the making sure you're
gone – which they had to do in front of
me – so it didn't happen as such. OK,
In truth I was staring at a Serengeti
wildlife documentary when the dying
didn't happen, quite the opposite, maybe
– nothing happened. Nothing began
to happen to you. Nothing happened
all through your organs and your heart
and brain and lungs and veins, nothing
happened to you. All over, nothing.

(Cheery, brisk.) My darling don't worry –
it's not that I was not paying attention: I
was. I really was. I *was* waiting for you to
die. That's how it was actually: you did
the dying while I watched lions humping
for a bit. And then the narrator – I recall
– uses the word 'disinterested' when he
means 'uninterested'. And that's when
I looked over at your at bed, because
now, you, you great facetious corrector
of grammar, I knew you would've liked
that! And that's when I saw you were
dead. Don't cry because you'll set me off.

LOUIS: I'm not.

BOA: So, how would you describe this – you
and me now? What do we say when
someone has gone, permanently, but
remains? Hey? Living, dead, just –
memory?

Because you'll never actually – be *out* in
the world ever again. I'll never bump into
you again. I'll never get a text.

But you are here, so I don't get it – the
funny thing is your airbag saved you,
but you got a bump from something and
then a little clot and then they got that
but during the op a tiny bubble of air
travelled to your brain and it's done this
thing. But you're not lost to me yet, any
more than the roots of a plant are lost,
they're not actually lost!

You're in here. *(Taps her head.)* And the
death thing's not – done its job, since.
What I mean is that the death thing
hasn't – been the be-all and end-all since
– you're *still* –

LOUIS: Oh Boa.

BOA: Your hands, your feet/

LOUIS: Guess I never got the hang of driving on
the wrong side of the road!

BOA: It was my fault we were in England!

LOUIS: No!/

BOA: I bet what happened is a fucking squirrel
or something ran across the road and you
swerved out the way.

LOUIS: I don't remember.

BOA: There was no booze in your blood/

LOUIS: Of course not!

BOA: You weren't speeding, the skids on the
road they think you swerved/

LOUIS:	It would've been a squirrel.
BOA:	We'll never know.

22.

BOA:	I've never told you about the ceremony.
LOUIS:	It better be good.
BOA:	Arsehole. All right, yes, your friends chose the music. Imagine my Mother sobbing her heart out to ska punk or whatever the hell it was, some reggae cover of Pink Floyd... It's a blur for me, the cremation. But I remember the beach. Jim to my left, unsteady on his feet. Val, my brothers, my mother sobbing in the wind, all of us with runny noses, a collie dog with a plastic boomerang that wouldn't leave us alone.

I was almost looking forward to the scattering of the death thing, because I felt – something would come – but – on that morning on the beach, instead of feeling a moment of release, of *scattering* you, and having all the pale ash of you in my hands – that wasn't the death thing it just wasn't – I was standing *there* – thinking 'Fuck there's *loads* of it!' We'll chuck a few handfuls off the Kent coastline and then I'll take you to your Dad's, and I'll chuck you in a kayak, I dunno, set it on fire like a Viking!

You never told me what you wanted, you dickhead! You always avoided the question. Only once you mentioned an ourobouros, or whatever…so for a while I was moving worms to the side of the road, in case….You know what I want, don't you? Fat lot of good you are to me now!

LOUIS: Yeah, I know what you want. Smashing magnums of champagne on the bottom of your damned coffin!

BOA: But Louis, I just felt a strange detachment – all of us were standing there, waiting for the right wind direction to take you and not cover us all! And I watched you, all ashy, float off, to be particled, but you're not gone, so I didn't really feel anything!

LOUIS: You're asking me to be gone.

BOA: I don't know what I'm asking.

All I know is that night we had a wake-type-thing at Mother's and then, when they'd all gone to bed I dismantled Hamilton Barksby and carried his bones in a crate to the bottom of the garden and I lit a shitty little bonfire…and I sat out there in the freezing cold dawn and burnt that skeleton. I was trying to make an ending, but I knew you hadn't gone!

LOUIS: OK. I know what it is. I ought to leave you with something. Oh god, my darling I can't think what to say, how to say it all? I can't think of any advice, I can't think of anything fucking profound! But – I think you are a great dancer, a great choreographer, and I love your heart. Boa. Keep moving people with movement! *(They laugh.)*

It's good. It's really good!

BOA: Still patronising!

LOUIS: Even the very worthy stuff you make about human rights violations! I think it's right…that one of us cares/

BOA: We both cared!

LOUIS: Yep but let me tell you right now… I don't give a fuck about any of it.

BOA: Poor Louis, eternally disappointed by humanity.

LOUIS: I mean it: I don't feel anything. I don't care what you do to this place or each other. My ability to give a shit about this place is gone.

Why did I stop writing Boa? Why did I? I gave up, and you never gave up!

BOA: We disappointed you. You said as a species we deserve to be annihilated.

LOUIS: God we're a pair of party-poopers you and I.

23.

BOA: I'm mad.

LOUIS: You're all right/

BOA: I'm not all right you dumb bugger! I've got nothing. I should have had your children. There *should be* your children.

LOUIS:	You're fighting. You're punching. You've got a show on out there! And you're the toast of the town! A Brit! And a *woman!*
BOA:	What's the point! You said you were tired of unwinnable wars; that we'll never learn! What's the fucking point?
LOUIS:	Listen up, my darling nihilist. We keep on living. And fucking and loving, and we fight this… 'society' to death. Drop the faux guilt and get your caboose out there.
BOA:	We're a bunch of pointless, prancing twirlies, you said.
LOUIS:	You're gonna go out, bow, and get a ton of flowers hurled at your head!
BOA:	I might just sit here and get pickled. Everybody's watching me. I can't get away from people's concern.
LOUIS:	I expect the amount you're drinking is the main source of people's concern.
BOA:	You're a fucking bore as a dead person.
LOUIS:	Come on, scoot!

24.

BOA:	But Louis – it's getting worse…it's supposed to get easier, it's meant to, subside but it's stronger than ever… Damn it, you said 'live with me forever'!
LOUIS:	I know.

BOA:	Then I missed it! I must have missed it! The moment when you'd be gone! I wish I *had* buried you, then there'd be a specific hole, and a place where I could go and lie down! I wish I'd buried you!
LOUIS:	Boa, you go out there and take your bow. The show's nearly down.
BOA:	I'm in agony.
LOUIS:	Agony?
BOA:	Grief, Louis!
LOUIS:	Grief is wonderful proof of having truly loved a filthy, rotten, stinking human being!
BOA:	I'm serious/
LOUIS:	So am I! You think I'm miserably rational but I happen to think the height of transcendence is to truly love another person.
BOA:	That's very poetic darling but I cry! Ceaselessly! See – my eyes have shrunk.
LOUIS:	Cry all you want. I promise it'll stop. But it's very, very important that you live.
BOA:	Why.
LOUIS:	'Cause life is so short, Boa. It's a butterfly's dream! It's a gnat's erection! Stop worrying if you ever did anything good in your life and just live it!
BOA:	Is this the meaning of life bit?
	(Exterior applause.)
LOUIS:	Go and get on with it! Go and be lonely.

BOA: What if I put my arms around you?

LOUIS: You saved my life.

BOA: Stay/

LOUIS: That was your cue. Off you pop!

BOA: Louis/

LOUIS: Boa. When you love

the dead

they exist –

in another category

All together.

Go.

End.